AT THE
FOREST EDGE

At the Forest Edge

C. Derk Janssen

CLARION'S CALL
PUBLISHING

Printed in the United States of America
ISBN 961-7176-1-06

Front Cover Art by Patricia Olson
Sketches by Devon Herrera and Patricia Olson

Clarion's Call Publishing
225 Cory Ave., Prescott, AZ 86303

C O N T E N T S

Acknowledgements

I would like to acknowledge and thank several people who have helped along the way in the creation of this book.

I'd like to say thanks to my family: my parents, Hal and Rosemary; my brothers, AJ, E, and Matty; and my daughter, Melissa. They have offered inspiration and support for many years. Also, I'd like acknowledge several other people who have assisted in important ways including editing and feedback. They include: first, Patti Olson, who has worked tirelessly for years to help make this book a reality - THANK YOU! Second, my friend, Don Iannone, who has offered significant insight and support. Also, a big thanks to others including Mary Jo, Pete, Janie, Lisa, Benny, the entire 400 Hall, Wendy and Linda for inspiration and energy.

There are so many more people who have helped me - I hope you know how much I appreciate your energy, support, and assistance. Thank you so much.

Derk Janssen
October 2008

This book is dedicated to my parents,
Harold and Rosemary Janssen,
two very special people of devotion,
love and courage.
Thank you for the journey,
and for all the love, dedication,
faith and strength.

Clarion's Call Publishing

Clarion's Call is dedicated to creating books that explore life at deeper levels. We strive to go beyond the surface, and provide perspectives that are connected, deep and meaningful. We encourage integration, compassion and healing - physically, mentally and spiritually. Our books focus on psychology, spirituality, green design, the environment, poetry, education and health. We believe a new day is coming, a time when there will be an opportunity to heal our spirits, our lives and the living earth. Clarion's Call is dedicated to helping that vision become real. We hope you enjoy our books, and that they provide some assistance as you move toward the fulfillment of your own dreams and potential.

Introduction

It appears that we have come to a crossroads, an edge, regarding our natural environment and the future direction of our society. It is becoming clear that we have adversely affected the ecology and health of our planet. Furthermore, it looks like many aspects of our lives - energy, building, transportation, over-consumption, materialism and health practices - seem to be out of sync with Nature and need transformation.

Research and studies are fine, but tend to live on the surface. What are the deeper emotional, spiritual and psychological reasons for our situation? How did we get here? Will we wake up? What are the forces that divide and confuse us? This book aims at a deeper exploration of these issues, and tries to offer some answers.

Derk Janssen
Prescott, Arizona
October 2008

Chapter 1

Starlight in the Trees

It is only with the heart that one can see rightly; what is essential is invisible to the eye.

Antoine de Saint-Exupery

deep within the forest

Deep within
the forest
where all is
still,

deep within
the forest,
where silence
and wonder
still live,

deep within
the forest,
where inner
passages open,
and the
rejuvenating power of life
pours in
and out,

there is
a deep sigh,
a deep breath,

and life,
deep, rich,
beautiful life
… is reborn.

Hear God

Down to the essentials,
stripped down to the core,

Down to the real,
To the inner flame,

To that center,
That place of honest, true,
  connected,
  and genuine,

Where we can feel nature,
Where we can hear God.

strong and deep

And the river
ran strong and deep,
blue and crystal,
but the current began
to pull in a new direction,

the sky was clear
and powerful,
the stars
were everywhere,
but their light
seemed somehow different,

mystery still lived
in the woods,
the trees still
connected us to long ago,
to dignity, strength
and courage,
but the eyes in
the darkness
had diminished,

change filled
the air,
different pathways
emerged in every direction,
choices,
battles to be won,

and
mother earth
and father sky
prayed for their children.

danced

I watched a tree
lose its
leaves today,

falling in
the morning breeze,

so beautiful,
the yellows
against a background
of brilliant blue,

the wonder
of cycles,
and patterns,
and timing,

one moment,
one beat,
one step after another,

and the moon
and the sun
danced together.

finally

a soft breeze,
blue skies,
trees swaying to the music
of the wind,

A bird lands
at the pool's edge,
takes a sip,
looks around,

There is quiet
and peace,
deep silence,
I feel myself breathe,
then more deeply,
and finally

... relax.

starlight through the trees

and the night
fell,
stillness
filled the air,
a deep calm
settled on
us,

we could see
clearly,
felt whole,
life made
sense,
there was
a plan,

and through
the trees,
sparkling,
we were
bathed in starlight.

bluegreen

a stone drops
in the pond,
and the ripples
touch the edges,
and my life
touches yours,
and yours mine,

we all
feel the water,
and we all
share the same
body of bluegreen,

we float,
we watch,
and we know
that the living web
connecting us all
to our precious,
planet
is threatened,

and we must
lift the mask
from our eyes,
and the bonds
from our hands,
and begin to fix,
and begin to heal.

Chapter 2

Set Free the River

Live life as life lives itself.

Lao-Tze

deep blue

Out of the blue,
   out of the mist,
   out of the everlasting deep,
Out of the ironies,
   and paradoxes,
   and hidden clues,
Out of the impenetrables,
   and the plan,
Out of the middle,
   and the edges,
Out of the pain,
   suffering and ecstasy,
Out of the deep, dark blue,
   every once in while,
   comes a burst of light,
   and a gradual awakening.

set free the river

set free
the river,
to flow,
to grow,

toward
the sea,
toward
the whole,

to untie
the knots,
and let
the lines
return to circles,

to unlock
the cages,
and free the animals
to join the woods,
and our minds
to join our hearts,

set free
the river,
to nourish,
feed,
to bring sustenance
to the land
and to our
spirits,

give data
and analysis
back to
natural cycles
and rhythms,

help prune
materialism and consumption,
and break
the fallacy
of
separate boxes,
let
the objective
and subjective
embrace again,

set free
the river,
and let
intuition,
heart,
wisdom,
once banished,
regain
their places
of dignity,

set free
the river,
so
we all
may heal
and be whole
again.

scurry

They move
to an orchestrated beat,
to ancient rhythms,
but drum beats
from far off
bring new messages,

discord, dark clouds,
they scurry for protection
and await an answer.

bigger swings

more fires,
stronger winds,
weather more intense
and unpredictable,

bigger hurricanes,
more rain,
less rain,
ice caps melting,
everything exaggerated,

natural cycles still in place,
but no longer in balance,
now with bigger swings,

more drought,
more hurricanes,
less food,
more disease,
fewer jobs, more anxiety,
… global warming, climate change, buzz words,
    market spins, real problems,

the bell is ringing,
nature is sick,
very sick,

too much growth,
greed and ego,
and not enough wisdom
humility,
… time to balance
    the scales.

sunrise

And late
at night,
all alone,
from somewhere
deep,
from somewhere
of anguish,

we pray for
healing,
for a simple,
connected,
wholeness,

for a re-connection
with the
natural,
with trees,
and animals,
streams and
stars,

we yearn
for a purging
of all artificial,
inside and out,

and to be one
with the vital force,
one with
the quiet fire
of sunrise.

light from deep in the woods

a glimmer
of light
from deep
in the woods,

the warmth,
the sounds,
the stirring of
deep
roots,

so much
connection here,
feeling
beyond words,

when the
invisible weave
is left
whole,
there is
light,
there is magic,
dreams and
spirit,

... life,
cherished for,

mysterious,
sacred,
...life.

to the music

rhythms,
rhythms,
moving,
flowing,
everywhere,
inside and out,

your heart beat,
the rain on a window,
and waves on the
shore,

rhythms,
rhythms,
beating,
quietly,
loudly,
invisible,
and subtle,

tall grass in
the wind,
clouds at night,
the moon is moving
and shining,
and we're moving,
and shining,
quietly,
gently,
to the music.

Chapter 3

At the Forest Edge

When we tug on a single thing in nature
we find it attached to everything else.

John Muir

at the forest edge

At the forest edge,
at the edge of environmental ignorance and ruin,

at the edge
of going this way or that,
we stand,

wondering, perplexed,
trying to move correctly,
because there may be little time left,

and all the while,
trees are falling faster
than we can count,
and being lost are the hands
and arms of Mother Earth,
and the healing of her embrace,
and slipping away is our connection,
our hope,

And so, what to be done?
how to proceed?

time to act,
time to help the trees,
and the frightened animals,
and the rivers
and the land,
… our home,
our Earth Mother.

softly

the earth is alive,
she breathes,
she feels,

She is aware,
she enfolds,
she nurtures,

When you cut,
when you chisel or pollute,
when you move hills,
you hurt her,
you hurt you and me,
and your children and their children,

So please,
walk softly,
walk softly and carry wisdom,
care and understanding.

hope

pavement,
pavement,
steel,
machines,
harsh noise,
and hard metal edges everywhere,

machines
and non-life
dominating,
separating,
dividing,
and beginning to win,

time to plant more trees,
time to bury more machines,
time to shrink the pavement,
and let the earth breathe,

time to let the energies connecting us
to the earth flow,
and let the spark and spirit
within each of us
flourish.

no measurable harm

a nuclear reactor
leaked today,
contaminating water,
land,
and crops,

barrels of
nuclear waste
were buried today,
and leakage from
them
will cause
cancer
for the next
100,000 years,

a nuclear reactor
partially melted down today,
exposing everyone
within 1000 miles
to lethal doses of
radiation,

the Dept. of Energy
released a statement
this afternoon
saying that no
measurable harm
has been done
and that nuclear
power is safe,
that low level
radiation is harmless,
and that there is
nothing to worry about.

and soar

we are one
with the rivers, forests
and oceans,

and we are one
with the sacred, the divine
and the soul,

all is filled with spiritual
energy
and all is connected,

we need to take care
of the living earth
and our physical selves
to create a
healthy foundation,

so that we can climb
into the higher floors,
so that we can
breathe, flourish
and soar,

we need to take care
of our home,
so that we can rejoice
and dig in,
and learn what we came
to learn,
and become all that
we can be,
and to get ready
to someday
fly homeward.

The Path Ahead

A young girl was walking along
the ocean shore one day, and she
happened upon a group of rocks
encircling a small tide pool. She
became curious, and so walked over
for a closer look. She peered over the
corner of one of the rocks, and gazed
at a fascinating little scene.

She saw a sparkling pool of water reflecting
different colors and shapes, surrounded by rocks,
some completely covered by water and some
popping their heads out. In the circle of water she
could see a starfish and a couple other creatures
beneath the water surface. They were shimmering
in the light, and she was hypnotized and calmed by
their beauty. The young girl could feel the sun on
her neck and back, and drifted into a kind of lazy,
relaxed place. She began to see more clearly the
colors, texture, and details of the tide pool. In that
quiet way, something caught her eye. It was the
sparkling edge of light from under one of the rocks.
As she looked closer, she realized it was the edge
of a box or case of some sort. She climbed down
from her perch on one of the rocks, and waded into
the pool. She reached down, and touched the edge
of the case. It was smooth, and she could feel its
curved contours. She reached further into the sand,
and lifted the case from beneath the water.

It was a simple looking container, made of smooth
stone. On closer inspection, it was oval-shaped,
with three individual stones embedded in the top.
It appeared weathered and old, yet had a feeling of
dignity and mystery to it. It consisted of two parts,

top and bottom, and was connected by an intricate latch, made of two smaller stones. She held the case tightly and climbed out of the shimmering pool. She found a clear, flat area of sand, and sat down. She held the bottom of the case, and tried to open it. It didn't budge - it seemed stuck. She kept trying to pry it open, but was not successful. She set it down to ponder her discovery, and the dilemma of trying to open it.

She held the stone box, and could now feel carvings in its sides, and a quiet comforting feel coming from it. As she held it with a little more respect, she seemed to connect with it on some level, and suddenly her hand must have moved the hinge correctly, because it moved and the box opened!

Inside she found smooth, beautiful stones, an old necklace, and a small glass cylinder. The stones were gold, amber, and a dark orange. The cylinder had a top piece, and a body of clear glass. It was about 5 inches in length, and about an inch wide. She removed the glass cap, and found an old roll of parchment. She uncurled the sheet, and saw some beautiful writing. It was old and intricate calligraphy, and she began to read. This is what it said:

"Breathe and be calm. Quiet and listen. There is a rhythm to all. All is connected. We live in an interwoven, connected whole. The forests, rivers, oceans, stars, people, animals, plants, sun and moon, mind, body and spirit - we are all part of a large, connected energy system. Intuition, dreams, wisdom and practical guidance can come from connecting to this living network. These connections are not just physical - they are also emotional and spiritual. Our communion with deeper pools of wisdom and spirituality is increased by our ability to connect, care and love. If we act in selfish or insensitive ways, and try to place ourselves in a separate and arrogant place, harm results. This can lead to isolation, loneliness and sadness. It can lead to valuing material things and earthly riches, but also in losing the connecting, revitalizing spirit. And it is through these connections - to the land, to each other, and to deep spiritual and emotional realms - that we unite with healing and joyous energy. We can then heal ourselves, our spirits, and our natural environment. Nature and soul are connected. Some have mistakenly imagined them separate, and that division has cost us, internally and externally. Ego and the false self are the dividers; authenticity and depth are the connectors.

The time is right to rediscover those deeper, connected realms. It's the invisible sacred fire, the spirit coming from the divine, that can connect, heal and guide us. We are all unique individuals, who are also vitally connected to all of life. We must do both - develop our unique and authentic selves, and also protect and nurture our connections to the land and spirit. In this way, we can find the Path Ahead, and a Journey of healing and joy."

She didn't understand all the ideas. The words felt a little strange, but gave her a good feeling. She knew she would read it again, but the sun was calling. The sand was calling. She drifted back to a quiet and re-laxed place. She was happy. It was a good day. She smiled, closed her eyes, and felt calm.

toward

we have come
to the edge,
environmentally,
spiritually,
politically,
emotionally,

time to choose wisely,
time to move away
from selfishness
and materialism,

time to turn toward
healing, humility,
strength
and common ground.

Chapter 4

Stepping Stones

If you find a path with no obstacles,
it probably doesn't go anywhere.

Unknown

like sand

Sand is rubbing
on us,
life is rubbing
on us,

there is friction,
pain,
suffering,
agony and ecstasy,

like sand,
life is rubbing on us,
and inside,
our spirit,
our soul,
is becoming
stronger,
and stronger,
clearer and clearer.

soil

take the pain
and transform it,

take your suffering
and learn from it,

turn it into
strength and wisdom,

take the cuts
into your soil
and plant new seeds,

new seeds
that will become
the plants and fruits
of a new
and improved
.... you.

gifts

our challenges,
our hardships,
and struggling,
are sometimes gifts,

and it's through overcoming
the hard times,
and rising above the obstacles
that we are allowed
   to climb higher
   to grow,

to become who we
   truly are,
and see with more
   clarity and wisdom.

reborn

moments
of light,
in continual
transformation,

living,
dying,
reborn,

new,
every moment,
everyday,

all around,
and inside,
we are.

soft wind

water splashes,
leaves fall,

your life,
moves,
inextricably,
often invisibly,
toward
your destiny.

all

spiritual lessons,
spiritual growth,
is all that
matters,

our body,
our lives,
are just the vehicles
though which
we are given
the opportunity
for that growth.

gymnasium

We are spiritual beings,
  our lives,
  our bodies,
  our circumstances,
  our challenges,

provide the testing ground,
the mechanisms by which
we grow,

they are part of a gymnasium
  by which our souls
  become wiser, deeper,
  stronger,
  more compassionate,
  and understanding,

... and closer to our true selves,
to others, and to God.

moving water

everything is unfolding
the way it's supposed to,
relax, but keep moving,
keep progressing,
keep moving forward,
gradually,
like water
flowing and
flowing,
everlasting.

transform

may your weakness
become your
strength,
may you
fill your holes,
and see your
blind spots,

may you
strive toward
completeness,
and turn
limited lines
into flowing,
connected
circles.

morning air

to live,
to try to live,
with courage
and bravery,
even when
fear lurks,
and tries to
grab hold,

to shut
the door
on darkness,
and walk
out into
the brisk,
clear
morning air,

that's the challenge,
the adventure,
awaiting us all.

remain constant

pain and
sweetness
intermingled,
up and
down
the waves
and tides
of life's
innate
orchestra
play,
and we rise
and fall
and learn
and enjoy,

and up
ahead,
if we stay
the path,
and remain
constant,
... finally,

light,
warmth,
and rest.

take time

In the middle
of pain,
in the middle
of suffering,
have faith,
have faith,
there's a reason,

There's a picture
bigger than you,
there's a course
of events,
and a destiny,

Try your best,
make a determined
effort,
but take time
to breathe
deeply,
to let yourself
connect,
to be at
peace.

unfold

Like a crystal
  unfolding,

Like a flower
  opening,

Like the first day of Spring
  beaming,

And birds knowing when
  and where to fly,

We develop,
  we grow,
  and on time,
    we unfold.

And Care

So many challenges,
so many difficulties,
trials and tribulations,

So, what to do?
How do we proceed?
How do we heal ourselves,
others,
and the living earth,

Maybe live more simply,
maybe more deeply,
in a more connected way,

Maybe move away from
the surface,
and so many things,
so many possessions,
and all the energy that goes
with them,

Maybe just breathe,
find a purpose
find meaning,
dance, breathe
… and love.

oh yes

to transform
all the bumps
and bruises,

all the hard
times,
all the dark,
deep, broken times,

into positive,
growthful
energy,
into new
direction,
into new
strength,

to re-assemble
all the parts
into something
better,
and to realize
all the good
that has happened,

yes,
through the trees,
and toward
the mountain,

we'll get there,
we'll get there.

just when

just when
you think that
all is dark,

just when
hope seems to
have drained away,

just when
bleakness is about
to cover you,

... the sun,
quietly,
slowly,
rises over the hill,
and warmth
creeps back
into your bones,

and a smile opens,
a trace of a smile,
from a newborn
feeling of "yes",

and even
in the desert,
a withered flower
blooms.

layer after layer

clarity,
simplicity,
layer after
layer
peeled
away,

until,
spirit,
heart,
mind,
and essence,

pulsate,
radiate,
flourish,

and we are
alive again.

life is opposite

life is opposite
she said,
and it rang true,

for we live in
a world
dominated by ego
and materialism,
by immersion in the physical,

But the deeper truths
and the living essence
is Spiritual,

And so
we continue to be
confused and lost,

And will do so
until we wake up
and see
that the physical is just
the surface,

But the deeper, essential
truth
is intangible and
Spiritual.

in the hands

it can be tough
it can be overwhelming,

the pain
and confusion
and torment
of the rough water,
of the trials and tests
we encounter,

but even in the
darkest times,
in the canyon bottoms
where bleakness seems
to overwhelm,
even then,
… we are in the hands
of God.

every moment

God is speaking to us,
every moment,
every hour,
every day,

All we need to do
... is listen.

"My teacher once said
	to me,

- become one with the knot itself,
	'til it dissolves away.
- sweep the garden.
- any size.

			Gary Snyder

"There is pleasure
And there is bliss.
Forego the first to possess the second."

Buddha

Chapter 5

Night Music

*The capacity to care is the thing which
gives life its deepest significance.*

Pablo Casals

silent depth

suddenly,
quietly,
there they were,
healing,
hypnotizing,

in translucent
beauty,
in melting
grace and depth,
the bluegreen pools
of her eyes,

flowing from waterfall
to waterfall,
nature
in silent depth,
running
over rocks,
through the woods,

and swimming in
those
deep, deep
pools.

flow of warmth

and my
arms wrapped
around her
in loving
embrace,

colors,
dreams,
imagination,
soared,
as I
melted
into a
flow
of warmth,

and became
one
once again,
in a
world
of deep
harmony.

lightening strikes

lightening strikes,
the poles are alive,
spark,
life,

blood flows,
the eyes
light,
magnet, conflict,

thunder crashes,
push and pull,
the storm builds,
and deluge begins,
and resolution is
possible,

clear skies,
inner calm,
    might be,
    might be,

man and woman
and the spark
and lessons,
are the seeds
for light,

for seeing someday
where the outer stops
and the inner begins,
where vision,
honed in battle,
is gained,

... in quiet light,
in loving embrace,
in mystery,
we grow
and learn.

flying dream

I had a flying dream
last night,
We were walking
through her
earthy, beautiful
home,
with arches,
rich colors,
and flowing, green plants
everywhere,

We entered a room
she thought we had
been to before,
but it was new
to me,
very high ceiling,
and dramatic fresco
painted on a
larger-than-life
far wall,

in paint,
city lights
and forests
all in one,
moving,
sparkling,
and then it all
came to life,

We held each
other,
she closed her
eyes,
and we were
flying,
and we flew
and flew,

It was the wind,
it was buoyant,
it was magical,
it was ecstasy,
and her smile,
and her hair,
and we kissed
and became one,

And we flew
toward a huge tree,
and I said,
shouldn't we fly
under, over, or
around,
and she said,
no,
we'll fly straight
through,
the limbs will bend
for us,
not break, just bend,
... and I woke.

blue sky

blue sky,
warm sunshine,
a walk in the woods,
holding hands,
holding each other,

sensitive,
kind,
patient,

fear dissolves
inch by inch,
and love is built
gradually,
slowly,
from the ground up.

stretched

let the mystery
build,
let the unknowns
feed your dreams,

magnet,
attraction,
eyes searching
eyes,
waiting,
waiting,
pulsing,
pulsing,

and then,
when the bubble
is stretched
and the air
so charged
you can barely
see,

then,
… speak to her.

touched forever

to catch lightening
in a bottle,

truth in a moment,

your eyes
in my heart,

and our souls
touched
forever.

to sail

I long for you,
your touch,
your smell,
your eyes,
yes, the sparkling, alive
fire
in your eyes,

I long
to feel you
to hold you
to move with you
and to let you flow
and trust me
and fly free,

to move
gracefully,
passionately,

to sail to other worlds
on the sounds
and rhythms
of the earth,
in the air,

and in the music and dance
we make
together.

communion

quiet,
  helping protection,
  hands held,
  a reassuring look,

support,
  nurture,
  kindness,

a walk in your dreams,
  a walk in the woods,

communion
  with the earth,
  and with higher places.

dance

I am bathing
in the movement
and the warmth
of our loving
embrace,

it's in your eyes
and your body
when we hold tight,

and move
together
in rhythm,

we dance
and circle,
weaving our eyes
and our smiles
together,

and gradually,
in sync,
leave the earth
and move among
the stars,

lost
in a healing,
loving,
dance.

to receive

languid,
sensuous,
mystery,
dark and deep,

secretive
and powerful,
   receptive behind
   a veil,
magnetic
   pulling, pulling,
hills waiting for
   the rain,
valleys ready for
   the river,

sky waiting
   for light
   to illuminate.

connect

sparks,
energy,
infinite expanding,

swirling,
evolving,
lights in
the sky,
and in
your eyes,

pathways glimpsed,
future, past,
present,
rendered
meaningless,

sparkling,
moving,
we share,
grow,
and balance
each other,

swirling,
swirling,
upward,
we journey
toward heaven,

and share this miracle
of life,
Earth,
and all
the currents
of life
visible,
and invisible,

the fire
glows,
your eyes
shine,
we look
across the
room,
and we
connect.

enter the water

dark,
alluring,
all said in one moment,

eyes
with desire,
without regard for safety
or boundaries
or others,

eyes
that said
disaster
and destruction,
but eyes
that said
enter the water
you will never be the same,

enter the water
and look into the face
of fear and courage
and all that
  could unravel
  and sink
or all that could
  be reborn
  and strengthened.

choices

spellbound,
hypnotizing,
startling,

the field lit up,
danger on all sides
our eyes met
and the karmic path
   rejoined,

transformation,
pain,
ecstasy,
... ahead
learning,
strengthening
but much at stake,

destruction,
volcanic fire
on one side,

and
release,
joy,
fulfillment
on the other,

... choices
choices.

unique roles

there are
different kinds
of love,

explosive,
fast burning,
and maddening,

slow
and gentle
and strengthening,

deep
brooding
and difficult,

friendly,
polite,
and light,

different loves
for different seasons,

different
dancers,
moving to
different
songs,
at different
times.

For Sale

Everything's for sale,
  your smile,
  your tenderness,
  your body,

Everything's for sale,
  your company,
  your time,
  your affection,

It's all on the table,
  "security",
  money,
  comfort,

And all you need to do
  is to put your life,
  put your being,
  your path
  on that table,
  and make the deal,
  make the trade,

... But then
  suddenly,
  you feel the sunshine
  and the breeze outside,
You catch a glimpse
  of blue sky
  and birds flying,

And something
deep inside,
calling, calling
you back.

rebirth

that smile,
those eyes,
that spark,

I am melting,
finally and completely,

and I flow
in a river
of energy,
of joy,

I finally connect
with the deep river,

and swim joyously
to the fountain head,

that place where the circle
re-connects,
and life,
wondrous, life
is born again.

and peace

the fire of transformation
burned hot
and strong,

and you were changed
you were strengthened,
and so was I,

and our eyes became
clearer and brighter,

then there was calm
then there was quiet,

the fire had cleansed
and purified,

then silence
and peace.

Chapter 6

A Small Rebel Force

Concrete is heavy;
iron is hard - but
the grass will
prevail.

Edward Abbey

still running strong

And there were
some,
and now more,
who left
the machine,

who left
the fragmented,
automated,
conveyor-belt,
way of living,

the way
that slowly
killed everything
sacred
and natural,

they left
even though
playing by
"the rules"
would have brought
"respectability,"
and money
and power,

yes,
they left
the pretense
the glittering
lie,

and they
were criticized,
ostracized,
and mocked,

often penniless,
and without
"respectability,"
and without
"approval,"
and standard
"achievement"
at prescribed
progress points,
they still knew
they were on the
right track,
they knew they
could turn the
tide,

because
they felt
they had discovered
some things rare and true,
.... wholeness,
integration,
meaning,

they had resisted
the illusion
of the short term,

of the tempting tributary,
and had found
the central river,
covered with
rocks in places,
but
still running strong,
toward the center,
connecting all
things,
in
healing
unity.

and then quickly

For the past 100 years
the model for much
of the world has been
  -- if it's economically sound,
let's do it,

What we need
is a fundamental change,
we need to be saying
  -- if it's economically sound
and environmentally wise,
let's do it,

If we don't make that
change,
the economic model
will have little meaning,
because
slowly,
gradually,
and then quickly,
the environmental will
  be lost
... and so will we.

to fight

Don't be afraid to fight
the good fight,

to fight for
honesty
and fairness,
and integrity,

for children
the earth,
the less fortunate,

for nurses
and teachers
and all the workers,
the salt of the
earth,

darkness and tyranny
are always lurking,
ready to attack
when things appear
vulnerable and weak,

And you must be ready,
you must be willing to fight,
and Light will help you,
and if you battle with
wisdom and effort
... you will win.

fervent prayer

we've given it over
to the merchants,
to the corporations
and the cash register,

we've traded spirit,
the intangible connectors,
and the truly spiritual,
... for things
and "stuff,"
for status and position,
for technological "advancements"
and surface sensation,

and meanwhile
community,
connection,
the environment,
health, wisdom
and spirit
... are disappearing.

we live in a 24/7 mall,
and all else is sacrificed,
this is a destructive
trade,
one that has led us to the edge,
a crossroads,
   the forests are being destroyed,
   the ice caps are melting,
   pollution is everywhere,
and all that is profound
and deep in our culture

is fading,
   and still we over-develop,
   and pave and shop and
   shop and arrogantly judge,

we continue to live in
the fragmented, separate
pretense
of the false self
and ego,

my hope,
my fervent prayer
is that we wake up
and wake up in time,

to regain our senses,
to come out of the fog,
and rediscover
the wisdom,
goodness and strength
that used to prevail
in this country,
and can once again.

much more

true wealth
has very little to do
with money
or status
or possessions,

and much more
to do
  with spirit,
  heart,
  caring,
  connection,
  … and love.

"A rich person
is not one
Who has the
Most,

But one who
Needs the
least."

- Anonymous

look no further

If you're wondering
where the neighborhoods went,
where the community
and connections went,

where the joy
and security went,

look no further
   than too many freeways,
   too much development,
   too much separation,
   too much impatience and greed,

look no further
   than selfishness,
   and insensitivity
     to the environment
     and the children,
     to safe, walkable,
     neighborhoods,
and the qualities that make life
special and meaningful,

time to come down
from the self-made throne
of arrogance and ego,

time to heal,
.... time for wisdom
and humility.

small rebel force

can we still be inspired?
can we still hope,
and see the best in people?
can we aspire toward high places
and ideals?

I hope so,
I hope we can learn
from dark places
and painful experiences,

I hope that
even in the face
of repressive regimes
and judgement, arrogance and hypocrisy,
we can rise above
and spread wisdom,
tolerance,
and a tough resilience,

Like a small rebel force
that must sometimes
retreat to the woods,
I hope that
we can become
flexible and forgiving,
and even
stronger than before.

the special ones

Some
are special,
very special,

something in the
eyes,
something in the
voice,
something in the heart,

they touch you,
they heal you,
they bring life,

and they're here
when we need them,
here to spark us,
here to bring us together,

here to make it magic,
here to make dreams
come true.

for Big Ma and Papa

the quest

to walk a path
of strength and kindness,
  of connection
  and individuality,

to take care of ourselves,
 others,
 and the living earth,

to be here
  and live with passion
  and yet no attachment,

this is the calling,
  the challenge,
  … the quest.

the flame

to leave the conveyor belt,
to leave the herd,

is to truly live a spiritual life,
because you are listening to
and acknowledging
the spark,
the sacred fire of life
that God gave you,

we all have a unique spark,
a unique flame,
and to nourish that,
to develop that,
to walk that path,
and follow it wherever
it may lead,

is to acknowledge and honor
that God is here, and that
He has a unique mission,
a unique plan
for you,

this way is
difficult
but very rewarding,
it is demanding
and arduous,
to leave the flock
the "security" of the group

and connect with
the inner flame,

this is a challenging path,
one that requires
discipline, faith
and dedication,

it is often misinterpreted
by others,
but it is a soulful
and rewarding
journey,

a way
of earthly simplicity
and frugality,
an emotional
and spiritual
bounty
of beauty and abundance.

fortunately

everyone has
their own
innate, unique
qualities
and ways of being,

just like snowflakes,
everyone gets their own
unique blueprint,

no one is a blank blackboard
to be written on
by external forces,

if that were true,
man would be
in charge,
… but
fortunately,
God is.

Find It

We are reaching the edge,
America has been losing its way
  and its soul,

And we will not find it
 by following extremists
 interested in corporate greed,
 war,
 arrogance,
 and everything being reduced
 to money and power,

We will find it
 in integrity and wisdom,
 by embracing common sense
 and common ground,

We will find it
 by opening our hearts,
 our minds,
 and by embracing balance and strength,

We will find it
 by re-discovering our roots,
 roots that once cared for
 children,
 the elderly,
 the earth,
 and working with our other nations,
 not alienating them,

We will find it
by caring,
and compassion,
strength and wisdom,
... and real leadership.

deep within our hearts

May the forest
return,
may the woods
come back,

May we begin
to see that
our roots
are tied to Nature's,

That all is one,
and that the
course of our lives
and our children's
will be largely
determined
by how we treat,
and how we
protect
the web of life,

And by how
sensitive we are
to the force
flowing
from the trees
and leaves
and animals,
and people,
and back again.

Chapter 7

Castle Walls

*The world has enough for everyone's need,
but not enough for everyone's greed.*

Ghandi

turns out

Turns out
that if you just give money
to the rich
and hope that it
seeps downward,
... it doesn't,

Turns out
that if you pander to
rich corporations
and hope they help create jobs here,
... they don't.

Turns out
that if you ignore the environment
and children
and education
and leave everything to the "free"
market,
and hope things will somehow
work out fine,
... they don't,

Turns out
that if you have no idea
about leadership,
or true strength,
or vision,
or principles,
or ethics,
or planning,

and feel that big money will
always bail out clueless and
mindless "governing,"
... it won't,

Time for change,
time for grassroots, innovative,
connected answers,
Time for each of us
to stand up
and walk toward a new day.

kindness and giving

I remember a time
  when money wasn't everything,
  when life was more
  balanced,

When caring for your neighbor,
When caring for our community,
When caring for the environment
  was important,

Somehow, some way
  we lost our way
Because nearly every minute
  of every day
  we think about money
  and selfishness,
  and the surface of the things,

I think it's clear that's not working,
Please, let's get back
  to caring
  and balance,
  to kindness
  and giving.

Gifts

It has nothing to do
  With the surface
  And with manipulating behavior,

And everything to do
  With nurturing and helping
  To develop the gifts
  That God has given
  to each of us.

And Love

Control
And analysis,

Technology
And domination,

Is nothing
Compared to
  Kindness,
  Compassion
  And Love.

A New Course

A Christian approach is not...

Turning your back on the poor and less fortunate,
Catering to the rich and powerful,
Waging an unjustified war,
Acting in an arrogant and belligerent way
toward others,

But that is what we've had for many years now,
Time for a new direction,
Time to chart
a new course.

Essential

Does the material, tangible, temporary
  world count?
... not much
it's here,
we move through it,
  there's dazzling colors, tasty treats,
  wondrous adventures,
  pitfalls and fool's gold everywhere,

Does the invisible, spiritual, eternal
  world count?
  absolutely,
  it's our core,
  our essence,
and the deep, true purpose
of our lives.

from the ground up

So much confusion,
so much disagreement
  about why our
  economic meltdown,

Look no further
than handing all the keys to the rich,
  who have only shown greed, arrogance,
  selfishness and ego,

Trickle down? Right.
  more like meltdown,

And some on the far right
can't wait to continue in this
direction,
... right over a cliff,

And the answer is,
this world is not flat,
  it is round,
trickle down does not work,
  we need to feed the roots,
  not the flowers,

Building the economy from the Ground up,
  and caring for the middle class
  is the only way to solve this problem,
It is the only way to create lasting strength,
It is the only way to bring healing and balance
  back to our people.

all the money

Give all the money
  to the rich
  and everything will be alright,

Give all the power
  to the rich
  and everything will be alright,

And then,
  look down and scoff at
  the middle class,
  children,
  the elderly,
  environmentalists,
  the less fortunate,
  the other nations of the world,

And then,
  downsize,
  outsource,
  exploit,
  rape and pillage,

And call it all the "free" market,
  and the righteous path of
  some on the far right,

And then,
  the results ...
  economic and environmental disaster,
  loss of respect around the world,

loss of freedom here at home,
  millions without homes
  and health insurance,
  massive suffering,
  lies, lies, hypocrisy
  ... and a fall from grace,

Time for a Change,
  time to Rebuild,
  time to Heal.

Yes and No

Yes to environment, education, the middle class,
small business, children, the elderly, the less
fortunate, renewable energy, solar and wind,
authenticity, love, compassion, negotiating with
strength for peace, sustainable development,
green design, resilience, strength of character, and
moving toward higher ground,

No to greed, narcissism, arrogance, urban sprawl,
the arrogant wealthy, nuclear energy, self-righteous
judgement, narrow-minded thinking, unethical
war, oil, surface illusion, disconnected living, and
trading your soul for the illusion of power and
status in the world.

For Some Reason

For some reason
  We don't seem interested in living
  In harmony with Nature,

For some reason
  We don't want to care, and nurture
  and connect to Her,

For some reason
  We want to be separate,
  And be able to dominate
  And abuse,
  And act as if the Living Earth
    is dead
    And there for our selfish and disconnected use,

For some reason
  We scoff and laugh and mock at
  those who do understand
  the errors of our ways,
  and who want to help heal and
  find ways to restore
  strength and rejuvenation,

For some reasons
  … maybe
    ignorance and greed
    and mindless profits,
    Time for a change.

Bush League

Amidst an illusion
of temporary
surface
grandeur,

amidst a
childish celebration
of greed,
and a "D" movie
version of
"leadership,"

amidst a
false picture
of "prosperity,"

... the country
went broke,
the environment
was raped,
education and
human services
suffered tremendous
loss,
thousands upon
thousands went homeless,

... and the rich
got happy,
and the party

went on,
the temporary was glorified,
the long-term was forgotten,

the surface
was polished,
and the people
were entertained,

while the depth,
and the substance,
and the real,
… withered.

Chapter 8

Circles

Everything the power of the world does
is done in a circle. The sky is round
and I have heard that the earth is round like a ball
and so are all the stars.
The Wind, in its greatest powers, whirls.

Black Elk

Listen

The stars,
The cycles and patterns,

God's sacred design,
 Everywhere,

Above,
 Inside,
 All around,
 All the time,

He speaks to us
Every minute
In so many ways,

... time to listen.

time to

We cover the
miracle of Nature
with pavement,
retail boxes,
and subdivisions,

We cut the trees,
bulldoze the meadows,
we smother
the miraculous, breathing
living Earth,

we disconnect
from life,

We alienate
and fragment our world,

We cut ourselves off
from Nature
and from our own
deeper essences,

and then we wonder
why there is so
much drug abuse,
violence,
and spiritual loneliness,

time to wake,
time to re-connect
to restore,

time to heal the
earth
and ourselves.

and let it

There is a natural
rhythm to life,
An unfettered, deep
eternal flow and beat,
A healing sound
and feeling,
One that is at the
core of all living things,

The modern world
buries it,
And it is a healing
experience to take off
the layers,
And let that rhythm come
back to life,
To feel, to become one
with it,
And let it rejuvenate you.

lightly

And so now,
  we stand perplexed,
  which way to go?

Perhaps, ... to live lightly
on the earth,
  simple,
  clean,
  humble,

to be strong,
resilient,
to care
  for the earth,
  and others,

and help
heal and restore,
  the earth,
  other people,
  yourself,

to be joyful
and humble,
to realize it's a
  miraculous and
  magical gift,

and it's a
great adventure,
  learning and
  fulfillment,

to connect with
and strive for higher ground,
heart and soul,
and to feel love
and express it,
... and let it flow.

wholeness

God created it all
and Spirit moves
   through not only
   our hearts and minds
   but also our bodies,

   it moves through the
   Earth,
   through the rivers, and
   meadows, the oceans
   and forests,

We need to protect
   and nurture
   all that God
   has created,

And we need to
   unite head, heart,
   body and Spirit,

This will bring wholeness,
   health
   and strength.

guide you

And so,
  what to do?
  how to proceed?

essence,
  simplicity,
  let nature take
  its course,

essence,
  simplicity,
  quiet
  and slow down,
  listen,

and then
  listen deeply,
  and let the Spirit
  guide you.

await

profound answers
and models
  await us in Nature,

answers about
  connecting with,
  listening to,
  and understanding
  the language of God,
  and the world
  He has created,

not the ego-based,
linear, fragmented,
separate, divided,
  world of man.

to life

the world
is a sensuous,
whole,
connected miracle,

a moving,
evolving,
organism of
light
and substance,

embrace it,
let the rain
soak you,
and the sun
warm you,

make your
mistakes,
and learn from
them,

treasure those
you love,
and hope,
and pray,
and work
for your dreams.

to live by

people are not separate
   objects to be used,
the land is not a separate, lifeless
   thing to be used,

our connections and relationships,
   to each other,
   the land,
   to spirit,
are not meant to be manipulated
for private gain,

they are sacred and need
   stewardship,
   respect,
   and care,

... lofty ideals,
platitudes,
unrealistic dreams,

... not really,
just principles and ethics
to live by.

the dance

the dance of life,
sun and moon,
fall and spring,

the flow of life fulfills itself
and then reverses,

life is extremes,
life is the edges,

but ultimately,
  it is balance,
  it is balance.

symphony

Every moment is
unfolding exactly as it should,
like the seasons
that come exactly on time,
we are all part of
God's celestial symphony,

All timed,
all in balance,
all connected,

It is not a random universe,
it is like the innate
unfolding and growth
of a crystalline structure,
there is a plan,
deep
and organized,
and innately engineered,

There is free will,
and it is connected to the plan,
doors that open and close,
options,
different pathways of
actualization
or not,

Connect with it,
breathe it,
become one
  with it.

receivers

We are but
receivers,
like radio transmitters,

we sometimes receive messages
from the divine,
the masterpieces of art,
literature, music,
don't come just from people,
... they come ultimately from
the Source.

it is called

God's architecture
is invisible,
eternal,
it is elegantly
organized,
perfectly organized,
it is a network
of energy,

and it compels,
guides, and
fills with intelligence
all that you see
on the physical
plane,
it is all powerful,

it can guide,
it can lead
  us to fulfillment,
  to peace.

eventually

process,
movement,
dynamic,
flowing,
change,

not static,
not fragmented,
not separate,

inventions of
the linear mind
give way

to
the glorious,
multi-colored,
dazzling
self-organizing
whole.

living patterns

There are
innate blueprints
everywhere,

nature is
perfect,

with swirling
timetables, clocks,
and patterns
unfolding precisely,

but sometimes,
people,
not in sync,
erect their own
systems,
their own inventions,
and often
wreak havoc
on the wondrous
harmony,

damming this,
stopping that,
accelerating too much,
depleting too fast,
believing that all is
arbitrary,

the time has now
hopefully come
when we can
begin to see
patterns,
the innate waves
and energy flows
touching and connecting
all living things,

time now
to free the rivers,
to free the animals,
to put things right again,

to allow
natural forces to flow,
and health and strength
to return to our lives.

pathway

the soul is that spark
that connects to the bigger fire,
the sacred fire,
  it is eternal,
  everlasting,

all else eventually fades away,
like props,
  weights and pulleys
  hurdles and obstacles,

the earth provides
the testing ground,
the practical vessels
  to test,
  to strengthen,

all is sacred,
the vessels are part
  of the divine plan,

part of how that spirit
  grows deeper, wiser
  and makes progress
  on its journey,

moves along the pathway,
  the journey
  toward heaven.

exquisite

human beings,
incredibly strong
and sensitive,
resilient *and*
fragile,

colors
pouring
from fingers,

invisible
intuitive links,
lightening
mental insights,
heart
embracing compassion,

a myriad
of living miracles,
brilliant
wonderful harmony,

so why do we
think that
x-rays to our bodies,
mercury in our teeth,
radiation in our food,
fluorescent lights,
engineered genes,
and chemicals
everywhere,

have no effect
on such exquisitely
sensitive instruments
as human
bodies and spirits,

why?
why?

mayhem

turn off your cell phone,
unplug your microwave,
reduce those x-rays,
move away from those
  power lines,
vote down that
  nuclear power plant,

we have surrounded ourselves
with a sea
  of dangerous
  unhealthy, man-made
  radiation,

everyone says it's fine,
perfectly safe,
a deeper wisdom
  shows something very
  different,

we have ignored the
intricate balance of Nature's
  innate,
  perfectly orchestrated
  web of energy,

and tried to replace it
with our own
  unplanned,
  clueless,
  excessive,
and completely out-of-balance
Electromagnetic Mayhem,

... time to wake up,
time to get back to balance.

and the gate opens

and the veils
are lifted,

layer
after
layer,

pain
brings
insight,

and the gate
opens gradually,

and eventually
the light
of what is,
truly,
going on,
inside and
out,

becomes
apparent.

Already Here

Imagine life
as unfolding from
the inside out,

Imagine that it is
sacred and innate,

that it is self-organizing
and perfectly timed,

Imagine that it is not
a blank blackboard
and that people do not
write on it from the outside,

Imagine that God has
imbued it with incredible
wisdom and sacred design,
and it is an unfolding,
sacred garden,

And that people and all
living creation
are to be respected
  and nurtured
  and developed,

Not indoctrinated,
   controlled,
   or "written upon"
   like software,

Imagine that our job is
   to awaken to,
   harmonize with,
   and help develop,
   the beauty,
   wonder,
   and strength

… that is already here.

Chapter 9

Passage to the Other Side

*We are not human beings having a
Spiritual Experience.
We are Spiritual beings having a
human experience.*

Pierre Teilhard de Chardin

coming into view

time
and timelessness,
and seasons,
and years
meshing,
and pendulum swings,
and meant
to be,
and living
a separate,
unique,
but shared path,
for reasons
once dim,
but slowly
coming
into view.

when we are quiet

We stand
between the old world
and the new,

between sunset
and sunrise,

events are moving
quickly,
we see them outside
and sense them within,

we stand in the
middle of vast
changes,
and look for
guidance,
for peace,
for clarity,

it is near,
it is inside,
and it is above,

it speaks to us
in instinct,
and intuition,
and shines
in brilliance
and tranquility
above the horizon,
it burns inside,
and speaks
   in visions
   in dreams
   in voices
when we are quiet.

learn

The American dream
of initiative,
private enterprise
and democracy,
is a powerful,
brilliant
and courageous
vision,

in most ways
it is working,
but too often
this
powerful engine
is insensitive
to the natural environment,
to working people, to children,
to the most fragile and beautiful
parts
of our country,

We must learn
how to balance
the powerful
and the sensitive,

the engine of business
and the protection
of nature,
the blending

of body, mind
and spirit,

we have not
found that balance
yet,
but we must soon,

so much
of what makes life
special,
magical,
secure,
is found in spirit
and in nature,

We must learn to
move ahead
with courage,
power,
and
with love
and sensitivity.

the whole room

everyone has something
to contribute,

a different candle
for the room of light,

just because each
is different,
doesn't diminish
any of the brightness,

we need all
the candles
to light
the whole room,

we need all
the perspectives
to see
the whole picture.

neighborhoods

planning
designed for
the car
has proven to be
a miserable failure,

increasing pollution,
global warming,
urban sprawl,
traffic, traffic,
alienation,
separation,
crime,
fragmentation,

what we need
is planning aimed
at the welfare
... of *people*,
planning that
strengthens downtowns
small businesses,
the environment,
history and culture,

planning that promotes neighborhoods,
connectivity,
more walking,
parks and community,

and that
increases
  quality of life
  for all of us.

more complete

Intuition is
    an immediate way of knowing,
    a holistic, deep way
    of understanding,
it integrates the mind,
    heart, spirit, and
    senses,

it is an immediate,
spontaneous
knowing and
seeing,

it has not been
valued by
our data-driven,
science-dominated
culture,
but may well
be a more complete,
higher way
    of perceiving truth,
    and reaching clarity.

never replaced

authenticity,
essence,
can be found,
by going deeper,

by giving up
fake, surface,
pretense,

by moving away
from societal status
and power,
and moving toward
deep, authentic
true strength,

true strength
can never be
replaced
by the surface,
temporary illusion
of it.

must end now

To think
that people are blank
blackboards,
and that only outside
influences
determine who we are,
is false,

All of us are *innately* unique,
we are all part of the
innate energy web of life,

part of the innate, harmonic, balanced
interconnected
flow of life,

to believe
that external societal forces
determine identity
is to place man and the
linear mind
on the throne,
is to place "control" and
science
on the throne,
this is inaccurate,
it is false
and at the heart
of many of our problems,

that is,
trying to "control,"
trying to step outside
the harmonic flow
and act as if
one can pull the levers
of life,
dam the rivers,
re-engineer the genes,
cover the earth with asphalt
and power lines,

build nuclear power plants,
introduce thousands of synthetic
chemicals,
re-program the people,
x-ray everything,
... is madness,

and must end,
if we are to heal
the Earth and all living
creatures.

lost

fish know to swim upstream,
birds know which direction to fly,
the seasons know exactly when
to come,

There is an amazing
innate design and organization
That is unfolding
in rhythm, on time,

To think humans stand
outside of that integrated system
is a mistake,
one that has led
to separate, isolated,
fragmented thinking
and lost lives.

seed & soil

The seed
is innateness,
and the soil
is the environment,

the soil
cannot change
the basic nature
of the seed,
but can determine
whether it reaches
its full potential
or not.

the attic

the goal is to link up
what we do
on earth
with our deeper,
authentic self,
and ultimately,
  our souls,

and avoid
crawling up into
  our attic,
  our ego,
  our fake mask,

if we succeed
we don't need
  so much stuff
  so much pretense
  so much false pride
  and ego,

and we can finally live
more harmoniously with ourselves,
with others,
with nature,
and with the divine,

and be more in flow,
in sync,
with God's plan.

fire

it's not just the earth,
it's the fire,
the spirit,
deep within
that connects us
  with the earth
  and soul,

it's the land
  the water,
it's the songs,
  stories
  and dance,
that come from
  spirit and fire,

it's the weaving together
that brings joy,
and it's that connecting
that's in jeopardy,
it's that blending,
that mixing,
that union of colors
and energy
that we need,

let's bring it back,
let's find a way
to reconnect so many
of the threads
that have been broken,

... it's time,
it's time now.

river

trading the False Self,
   ego, pretense, status, money, things,
   things, surface and fake,

for the Real Self,
   authentic, connected, deep, true,
   honest, humble, strong and real,

is a foolish and dark trade,
one that has cost this country,
this world,
and millions of people
dearly,

time to take off the armor
and the mask,
time to get out of the separate,
fake, artificial box,

and get in the river,
time to get wet,
and then bask in the warmth
of natural sun,
and the comforting
beach.

In The Woods

I was deep in the woods one day, and came upon an old, bearded man. He lived in a small, almost entirely hidden little cottage. It was nearly buried by trees and bushes, but his porch was in plain view,  and that's where I saw him sitting. He was smiling, and just watching the day go by. I walked up and started speaking to him.

We had a pleasant conversation, nothing in particular. He smiled and spoke in simple little phrases. I can't remember all that he said, but I do remember one part of our conversation. I asked him how long he had lived there, because it seemed that he had been there for a long time. At first, he looked away and seemed to focus on a tree or a bird or something in the sky. Then he spoke slowly and clearly, " The most important thing about time is that it's much different than what we think. It doesn't go in a straight line, it flows in circles and is alive." I was a little confused, and asked him to clarify. He continued, "The most important things in life can't be seen, they are felt. You see, time flows, and nothing is separate. Things move in circles, and there is timing, there are reasons and seasons for everything. There is the surface of how things might appear, and then there is the depth, the truth of something … a tree, or a bird, or a person, like you."

Now I was really confused and didn't know how to reply, because now I was somehow in his story. But he kept going anyway, " I've been here for awhile, but you know, you can be somewhere for a year one day, and somewhere else for a day one year. The truth, the deep truth of a situation, is maybe somewhat different than how it appears. Actually, sometimes life is opposite." That startled me, and I replied, " What did you just say – life is opposite? What does that mean?" He smiled, and said, "What I mean is that what's on the surface sometimes acts like a mask. The surface often doesn't express what's actually, truthfully going on deep inside. And the more modern life seems to go, the bigger that difference becomes. More and more, people seem to be faking it … not being who they truly are, and we end up with life being opposite, the surface being very different than the real truth." I said, "How do you know these things? It seems like you've been isolated back here for a long time, out of touch with things." He smiled, and replied, " See, I told you, life can be opposite - I see, I feel, I understand some things… Now you take care sonny, and have a great day. And remember, don't just look, see with your heart and your mind's eye. There's a lot going on out there, and most of it is below the surface."

I said goodbye, and walked on down the path. I should have been really confused, but somehow, in some way, what he said made sense. Some clouds moved in, and it began to softly rain. The light in the woods was almost magical, mixing darkness and light, sun and water… and I started to feel relaxed. It was a good day, he might be onto something… we'll see how it goes.

interwoven

And through all
they differences,
they searched for
common ground,

they searched for
that place,
down deep,
where they were
connected,

beyond the surface,
beyond the frailties,
and imperfections,

where they were
woven
to each other,
to the land,
and to the force
that binds,

beyond different
perspectives,
beyond different
opinions,
toward that place
where we
are one.

Chapter 10

Seeds in the Wind

*You must be the change
you want to see in the world.*

Mahatma Ghandi

green

trees,
trees,

mystery
and love
and the air
we breathe,

our
ancient
friends,

roots
and parents
and grandparents
and children
and leaves,

protection,
shade,
and nurturing,
and all that is
whole
and strong,

forests
and trees
and the threads
connecting
all of us.

exactly

The current environmental/energy/
  economic crisis
is both a challenge
and an opportunity,

We need to move toward
  a Green World,
and this transformation
is a great business opening,
a significant health opportunity,
and a wondrous chance
for the world to come together
  to find solutions,
  to find harmony
  and cooperation,

A coming Green Challenge
  might be
  exactly what
  we need.

Together

If we need something
  To help bring us all together,

Perhaps it is the survival
  Of Mother Earth,
Perhaps it is the health
  Of our living planet,

Can we meet
  in the middle,
  and talk and discuss,

And create Solutions
  that are positive and constructive
  and achieve common ground,

The time has come to shake hands,
  to share ideas,
  to paint together
  on a new canvas.

To Heal

The essential problem is this:
to trust only the tangible,
only that which can be
  measured,
  weighed,
  tasted, touched,
  and put in bank accounts,

To trust
  only that which can be
  analyzed and dissected
  is not the way,

The pursuit,
  the accumulation of physical things
  will destroy the earth
  and will never satisfy,

We have been led astray
  we have been fooled
  by the physical,
  the tangible,

We need to simplify, simplify
  and follow
  our hearts,
  our intuition,
  our connection to God,

And that is all invisible,
  and actually much more real,

Because that simple path
  has the power
  to connect,
  to cleanse,
  and to heal.

Roots & Flowers

To unlock the potential
of our mind, our body,
our spirit,

is a quest
an adventure,
an exploration,

... that never ends.

Seeds

Some of us were made ... not to fit into the
traditions of this culture,

...but to be the seeds for a new one.

part of the process

If you have *not* found
your true, authentic self
and life purpose,

Then you will need
lots of money
and things
and false status
to compensate
for that large hole
in the center of you,

Because essence,
authenticity, purpose and God
are the only things
that will bring you peace,
security and contentment,

And actually,
finding authenticity and purpose
is connected to
finding God.

forward

Follow your
intuition,

you may not
end up fitting
into what is,
today's conveyor belt
may not be for you,

Follow your intuition,
and you may very well
fit in with what
will be,
and the world you
can help create.

new course heading

we need a
great leap of awareness,
a leap of
change,
and new
direction,

and it's not
more science,
it's not
more linear dead ends,

it's joining,
it's integration,
  a connection
  of our hearts
  and our minds,
  of nature
  and people,

and an awakening
to the richness,
complexity
and marvel
of how
we are intertwined
with the rhythms,
cycles,
and clockwork
of the natural world.

"development"

freeways,
urban sprawl,
more and more
"development"

it costs communities
   increased taxes,
   loss of nature and culture,
and creates
   a fragmented, alienated
   world of pavement, retail boxes,
   traffic congestion,
   and lifeless, artificial,
   disconnected places,
where our children lose hope,
where most of us lose beauty, quality,
depth and peace,

while the few,
   who glorify greed and selfishness
   get "rich"
   and ultimately
   ... miserable,

time for a change,
time for return to quality
   over quantity,
and for wisdom and balance
   to replace
   immediate and separate.

revival

We need a Revival,
a true, rejuvenating
deep spiritual re-awakening,

not a fake, arrogant,
hypocritical side-show,

we need an authentic
soul-searching rebirth,
we need humility
and vision,
and a true journey toward
higher ground,

we don't need
self-righteous, judgement,
fear and division,

we don't need lies
and surface smiles,

we need true caring and compassion for
  the poor, the downtrodden,
  the needy and all the families
  with no money
  or insurance
  or hope,

we need to care for the
  living earth,
  for the rivers, the oceans,
  the forests,

and all the connections
between nature
and our hearts, mind and souls,

We do not need corporate
hand-outs and bailouts,
and the fake surface
of judgement, "morals" and "ethics"
that are based on
division, fear and archaic
aristocratic pretense,

We need to go deeper,
and find true compassion
and wisdom,
we need to meet in the middle,
at a deep and real place,
to lead our people
toward health and strength.

Chapter 11

Quiet Meadow

Less and less you need to force things
until finally you arrive at non-action
where nothing is done, nothing is left undone...
The Master does nothing yet...
leaves nothing undone.

Lao Tze

Listen

You can't hear God
If you're moving too fast,

Slow down a bit,
Breathe,
B r e a t h e,
Feel,

Quiet yourself,
Slow yourself down,
... and listen.

Breeze

Summer breeze,
Birds splash in the bath,

The trees whisper
  and then sing,
The wind cools
  and soothes,

The colors, moods and flow
  of the forest floor,
Alive, at peace,
  in harmony,

My mind begins
  to quiet,
I begin to feel
  once again.

a new course

Today
I plotted a
new course,
I had a
new vision,
A vision of faraway
places,
and a home for my heart,

A home of blue and
corral and warm
yellows and reds,
a home of quiet, and
caring, and balance,
a home,
... a home for my heart.

whole again

slow,
gradual,
peaceful,

rest,
sunlight,
a walk in
the woods,

simple,
whole foods,

the soft
rhythm of
music,

slow down,
slow down,
deep, deep
breath,

quiet, quiet,
... healing.

love one

trees,
trees,
the limbs,
of mother earth,

reaching out,
protecting,
giving,

shelter,
air,
majesty,
beauty,

drama,
and mystery,
and life,

we need them,
we need them,
we need to begin
protecting those limbs,
her trees,
our trees,

they are the boundary,
the definition,
the metaphor and the reality
of our survival,

please,
please,
plant one,
save one,
cherish one.

A Hole in the Middle

Selfishness,
fake illusion,

Accumulation
Of physical stuff,
mindless materialism and ego,

They are hollow
 and will not fill the essential center,
 where Spirit, Authenticity and Purpose
 belong,

The Center will not accept the wrong material,
 it needs the real deal,

Time to turn from illusion,
Time to turn from surface and ego,

And find Authenticity, Purpose and Spirit.

slow down

When life is about money
and economics
  the pace quickens,
  the focus is on the surface,
  and we tend to use up the earth
  and abuse it,
  and pollute it,

When life is more about spirit
and caring,
  we go slower and deeper,
  and find more meaning and
  contentment,

We also tend to actually take care
  of the earth and each other,

Slowing down is good,
  breathe,
  breathe …
  go deeper,
  find healing for yourself,
  the earth,
  and all living beings.

in you

nothing like stars
to fill you
with wonder and magic,

nothing like stars
to give you
hope and let
you dream,

nothing like stars
on a brilliant
clear night
to let you feel
fresh and new
and reborn,

nothing like stars
to bring you
perspective
and balance,
and erase your worries,
to bring joy
and sparkle to your eyes,

don't forget
that sparkle,
it's up there,
... and it's *in*
you.

Chapter 12

Toward the Mountain

And what do you benefit if you gain the whole world
but lose your own soul?

Jesus Christ

choosing

We're at
the crossroads,

spirit or matter,
process or content,

compassion or judgement,

time to see,
time to choose,
time to heal.

what we need

.

too bad
about the "information" age,

what we need
is the "wisdom" age.

alive

The earth is alive,
all living creations are connected,
nothing is blank,
all is imbued with innate,
unique and sacred design,

Time to awaken
to the intricate balance
and innate energies
all around and inside of us.

Communion

Communion with nature,
Communion with God,

to feel with your heart
   your Spirit
   and through your body,

To connect
   and open your center,
   your heart,

to listen to God,
   and follow His Words,
   to find wisdom
   and vision,

this is the way to
   move away from the forest
   edge,
away from environmental
   destruction,
away from greed and selfishness,
... toward balance
   and healing.

soul food

We are not essentially
  physical,
we are essentially
  spiritual,

and our world
  is a school,
  a soul school,
created and structured
  for soul growth,

yes, it's full of physical
  things,
powerful physical things
  and forces,
but they pale in comparison
  to the strength and endurance
  of the Spiritual,
  to the soul essence
  of our world,
and what is inside
  of us,

it is like a gym,
we are working out,
and it looks like
we're working the body,
but that's just the
   surface,

we are working on
   something deeper,
   and far more important,
we are striving to improve
to strengthen,
   to grow
... our soul.

my hope

To sell your soul
to gain the world
is at the center of
darkness,

America is close to
that place,
valuing materialism,
narcissism, ego
and power,

it is threatening
  our center,
  our integrity,
  our health,
  and our essence,

it is not just the
natural environment
that is threatened,
  it is our spirit,
  our character,
that is weakening,

we have come
to the edge,
to a crucial crossroads,
and we must pause
and think,
and find wisdom,

as we strive for light
and guidance,
it is my hope,
my prayer,
that writers write,
and singers sing,
and people speak up,

and that these little
poems help,
and all the books help,
and all the songs help,
by all of us,

and are spread,
until we have
the strength
and union needed
to turn the tide
and move in a new direction,
a path of clarity,
  strength and wisdom.

wondrous difference

We're coming
to the mountain
from different directions,

We're coming
to the light
by different roads,

if we could just
open our eyes
and our hearts,

And welcome
all the wondrous
diversity.

next

The next Revolution -
  Spirit, Green
  and Connected,

  not ego, fake
  and separate.

sacred

It's all sacred
    and it's all connected,
    the earth
    the body
    mind
    and spirit,

division is the problem
… integration and balance are the answers.

for children

There needs to be
   somewhere for children to play,

Somewhere to feel joy
   to see blue sky
   to feel trees
   and run in the fields and flowers
   of Mother Earth,

Somewhere to feel alive
   and strong,
   and connected,

Protect, preserve
   the sacred earth,
That is our mission,
   that is our goal.

reborn

moments
of light and Spirit
in continual
change,

living,
dying,
reborn,

new,
every moment,
everyday,

all around
and inside,
we are
moments
of light,
in dance
in celebration
in transition,

we are channels
of Spirit
turning and
changing
... always.

toward the mountain

Toward the mountain,
through the physical
  we move toward Spirit,

Through trials and tribulations,
  we move toward healing,
After division and ego
  and fake,
We move toward depth,
  meaning and connections,

We are on a journey,
  we are guided
  we are challenged
to move Forward
  toward the Mountain.

starlight

In the
stars at night,
there is clarity,

In the
stars at night,
there is vision
and dreams,
and a glimpse
of what the world
could be,
… and of what you
could be,

In the
stars at night,
magic is reborn,
and so are we.

Time is Now

Time to touch,
time to feel,
Time to connect,

We have come to an edge,
and we can
choose,
we can act
wisely,

The river calls,
The forest beacons,
The oceans, trees, animals and
  children call out,

Listen,
Feel,
Connect,

You can do it,
We can do it,
... the time is Now.

Font:
Palatino

Paper:
70# Finch Vanilla Opaque

Printed by:
Allegra Print & Imaging
Prescott, Arizona

CLARION'S CALL
PUBLISHING

For more information about
Clarion's Call

please write to:
Clarion's Call Publishing
225 Cory Avenue
Prescott, AZ 86303

or visit our website at:
www.clarionscall.net